THE MET

AMAZING TREASURES

COLORING BOOK

Editor Satu Hämeenaho-Fox
Designer Emily Portnoi
Project Editor Rosie Peet
Picture Researcher Martin Copeland
Production Editor Siu Yin Chan
Production Controller Louise Minihane
Senior Acquisitions Editor Katy Flint
Managing Art Editor Vicky Short
Publishing Director Mark Searle

First American Edition, 2022
Published in the United States by DK Publishing
1745 Broadway, 20th Floor, New York NY 10019

Page design copyright © 2022 Dorling Kindersley Limited
DK, a Division of Penguin Random House LLC
22 23 24 25 26 10 9 8 7 6 5 4 3 2 1
001–334151–Nov/2022

The Metropolitan
Museum of Art
New York

ISBN 978-0-7440-6346-2
DK books are available at special discounts when
purchased in bulk for sales promotions, premiums,
fund-raising, or educational use.
For details, contact: DK Publishing Special Markets,
1745 Broadway, 20th Floor, New York NY 10019
SpecialSales@dk.com

Printed and bound in China

For the curious
www.dk.com
www.metmuseum.org

THE MET

AMAZING TREASURES

COLORING BOOK

REVEAL WONDERS
INSPIRED BY MASTERPIECES
FROM THE MET COLLECTION

ILLUSTRATED BY
MEGHANN RADER

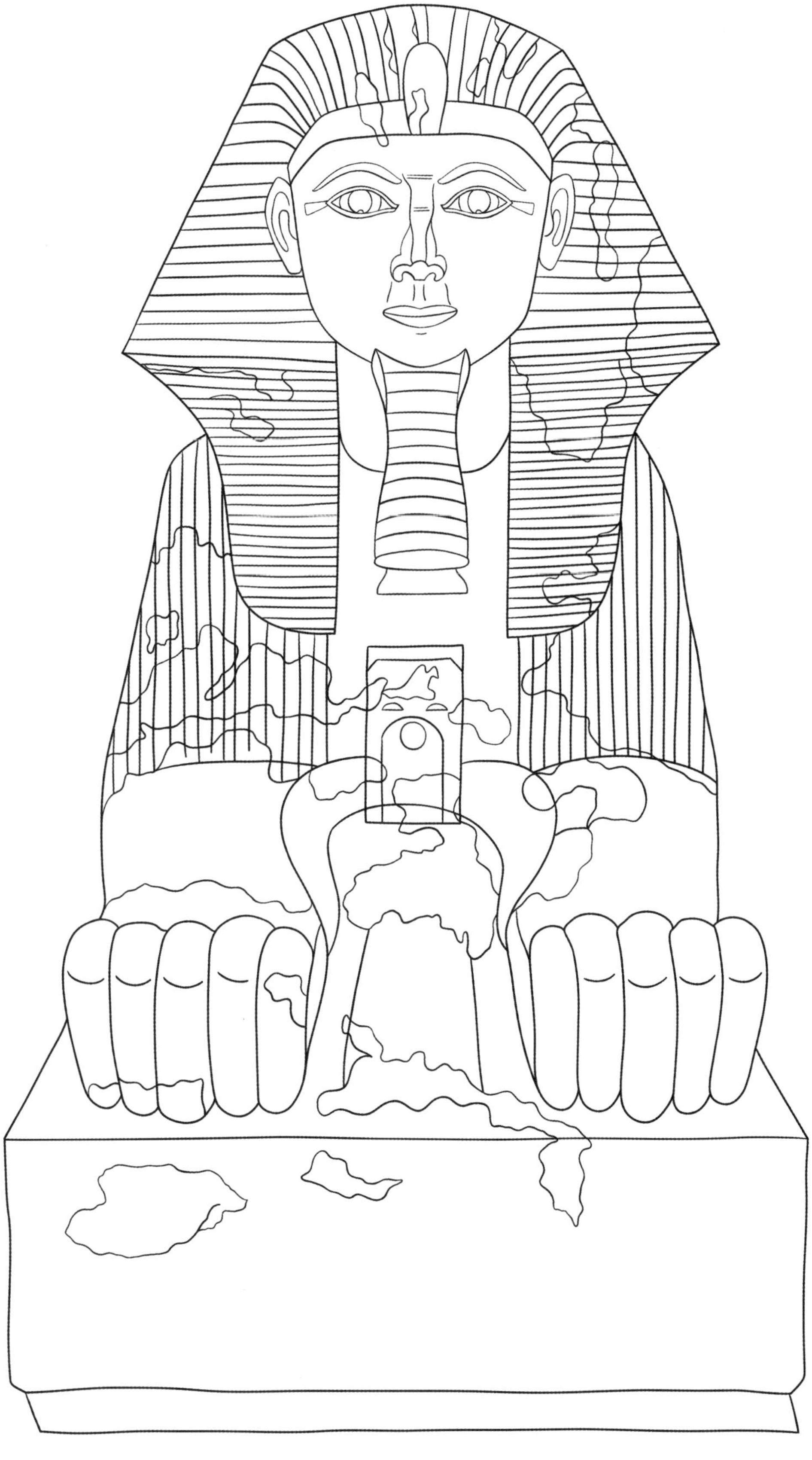

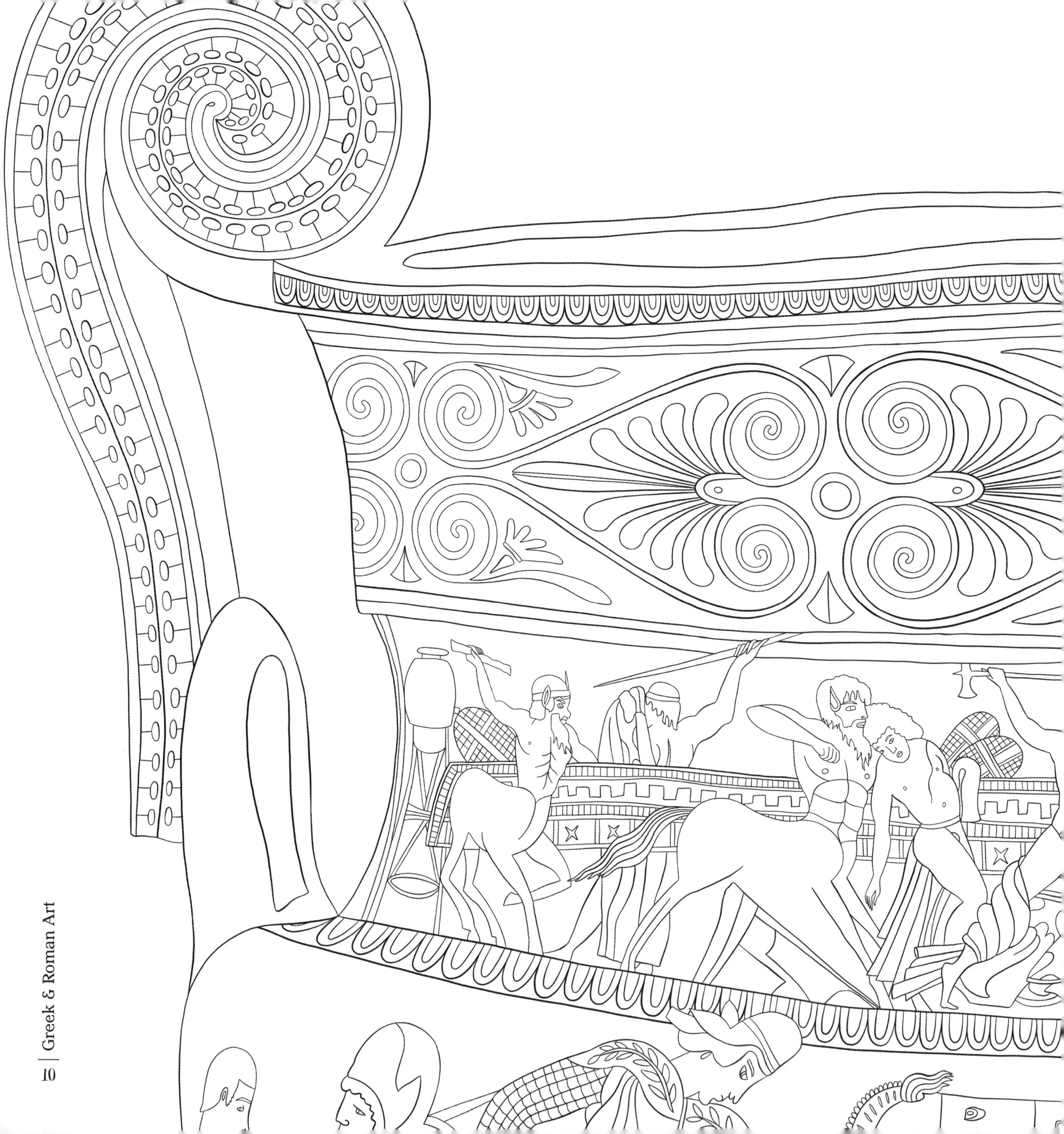

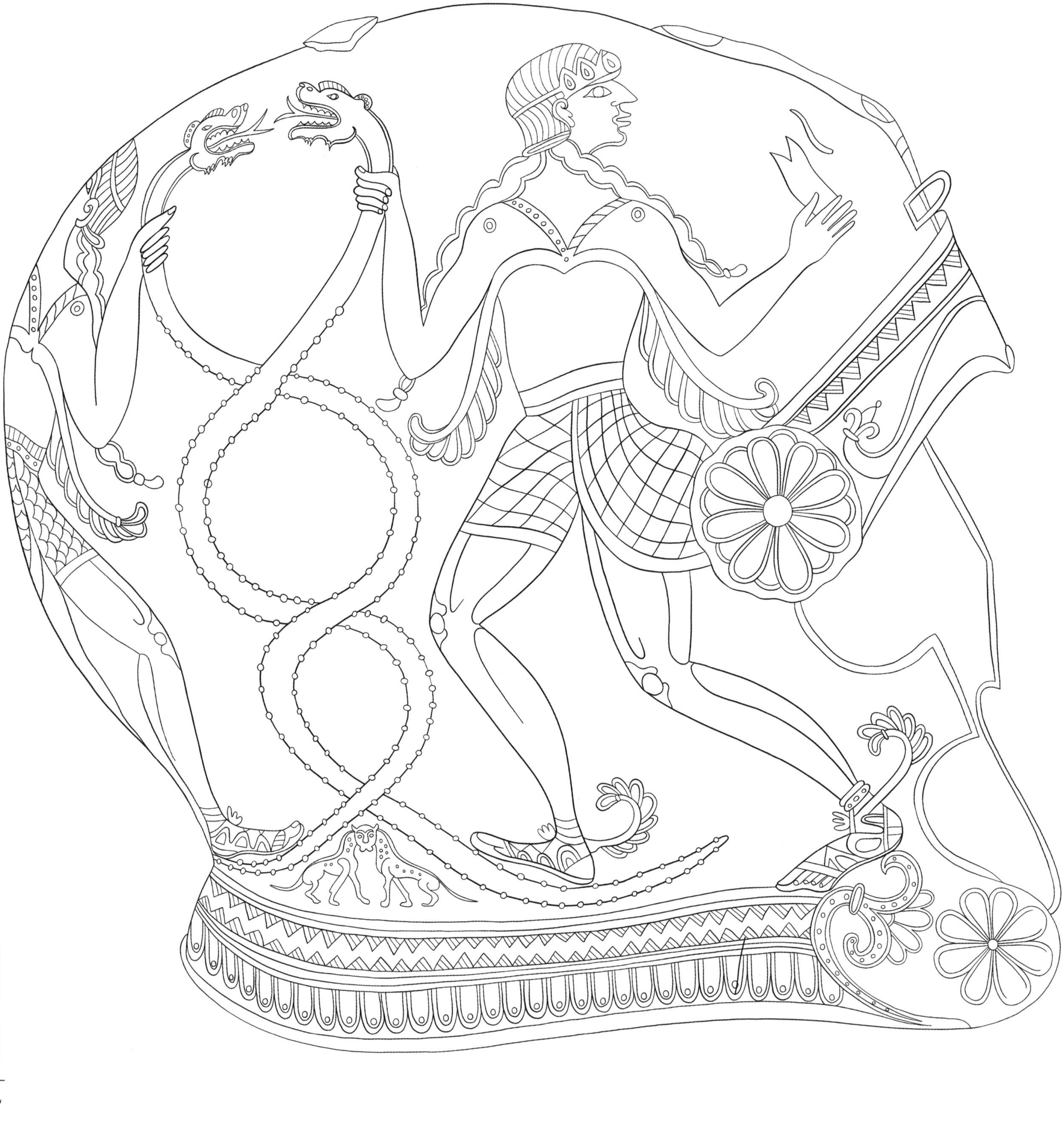

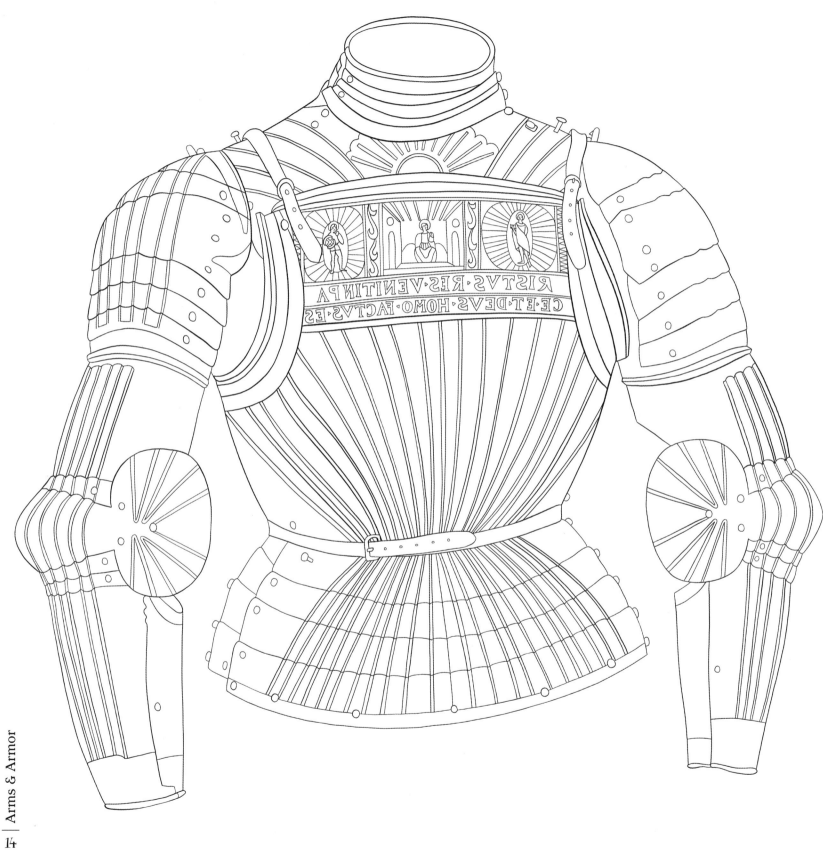

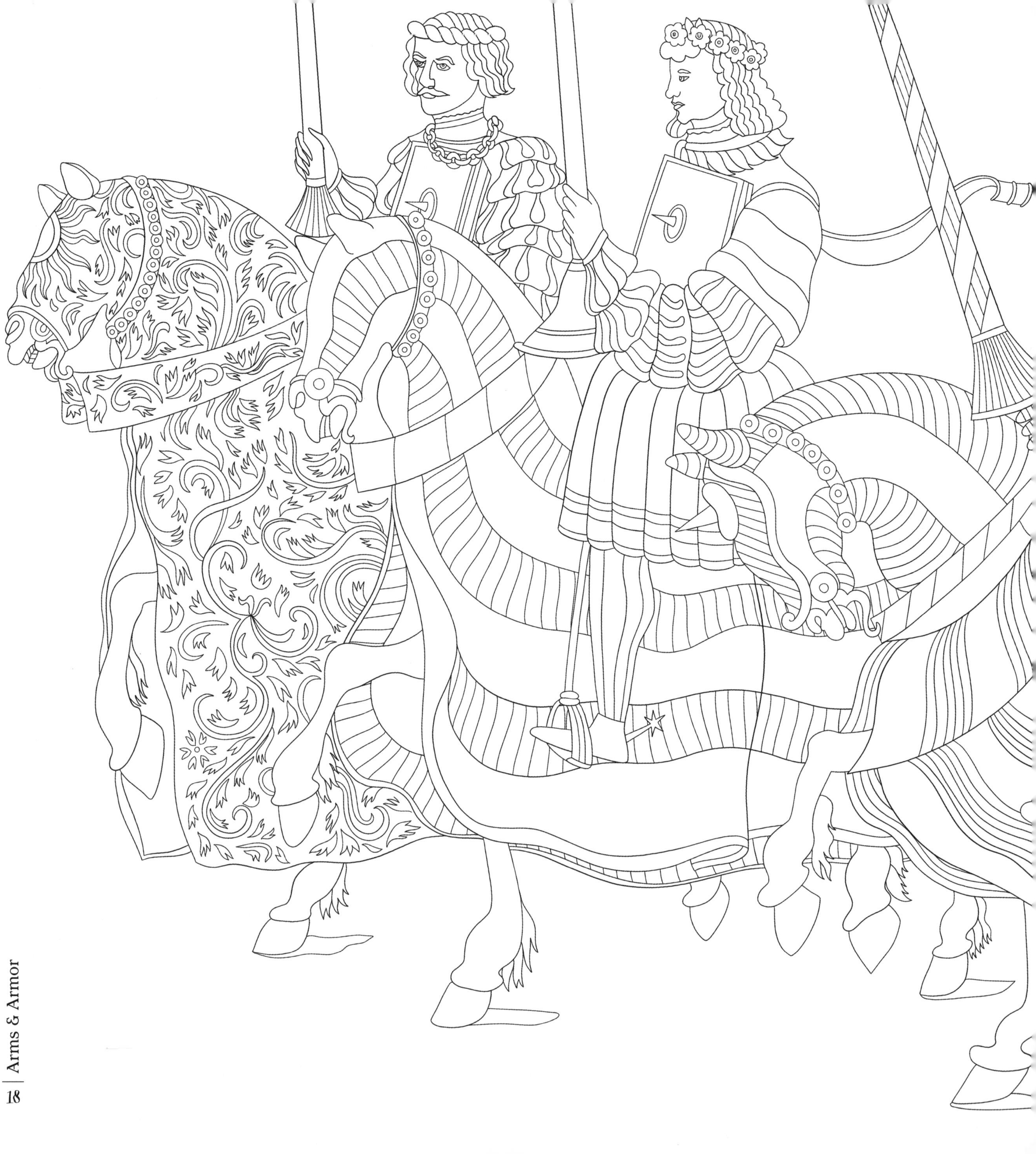

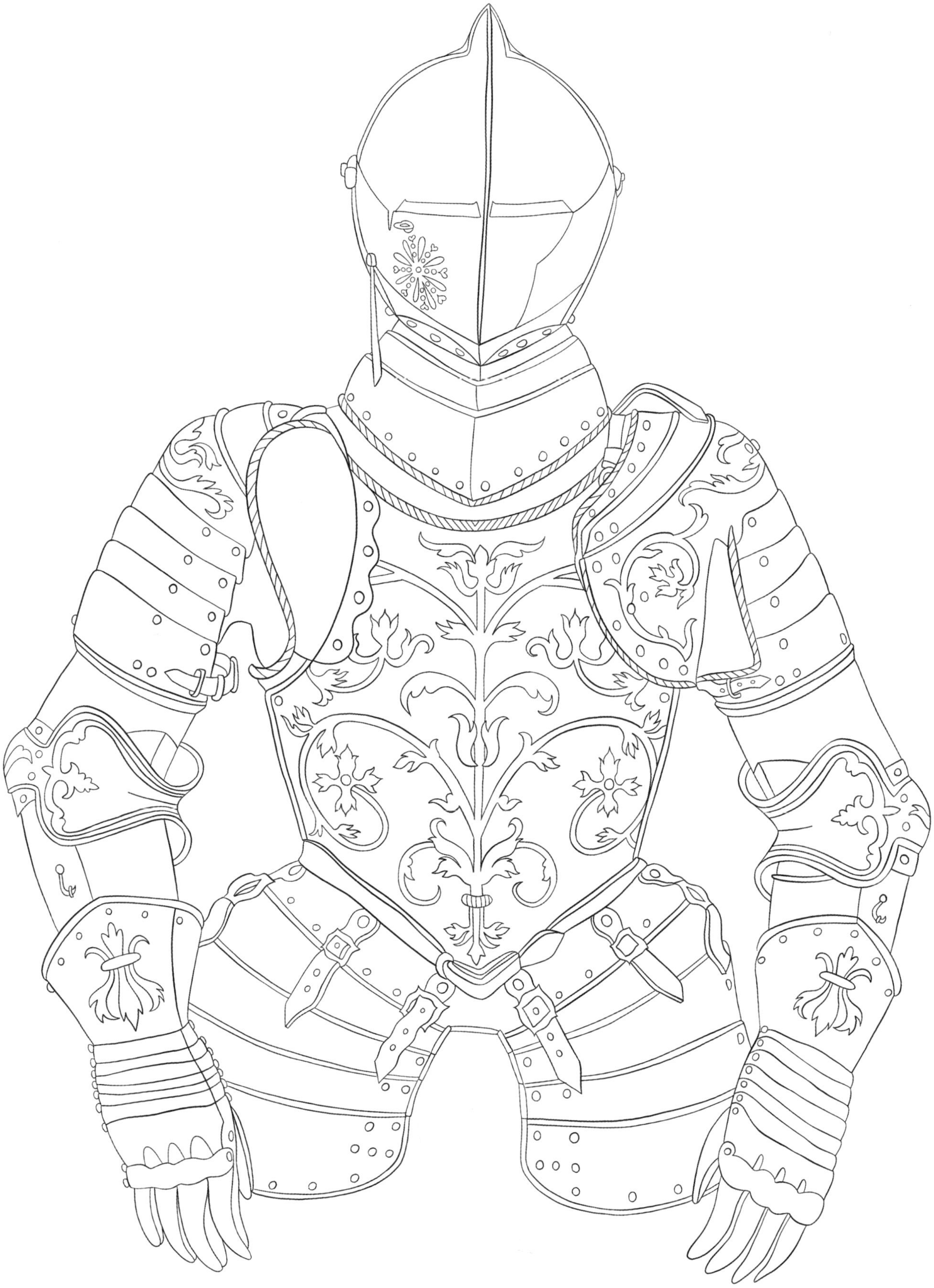

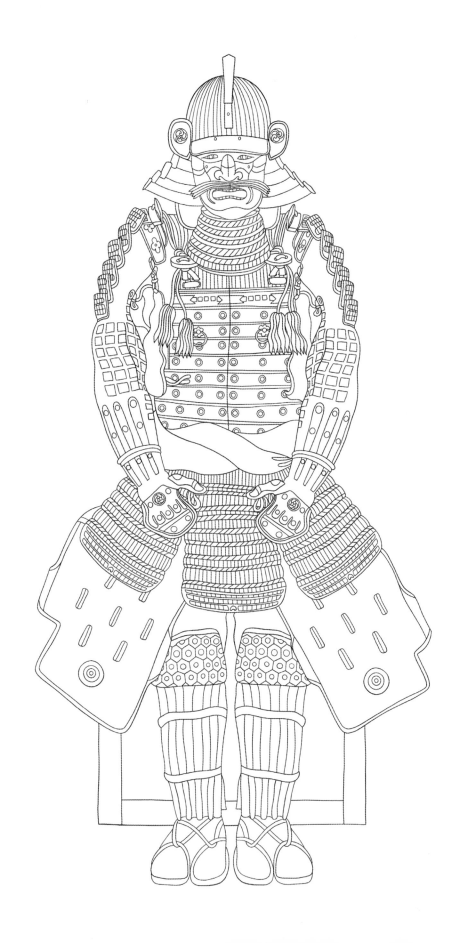

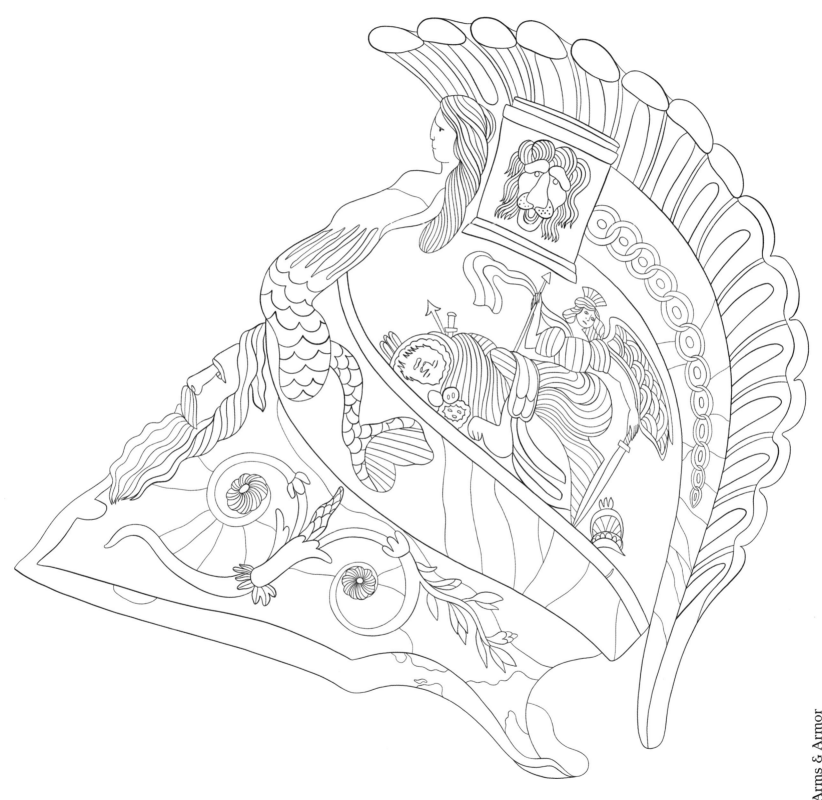

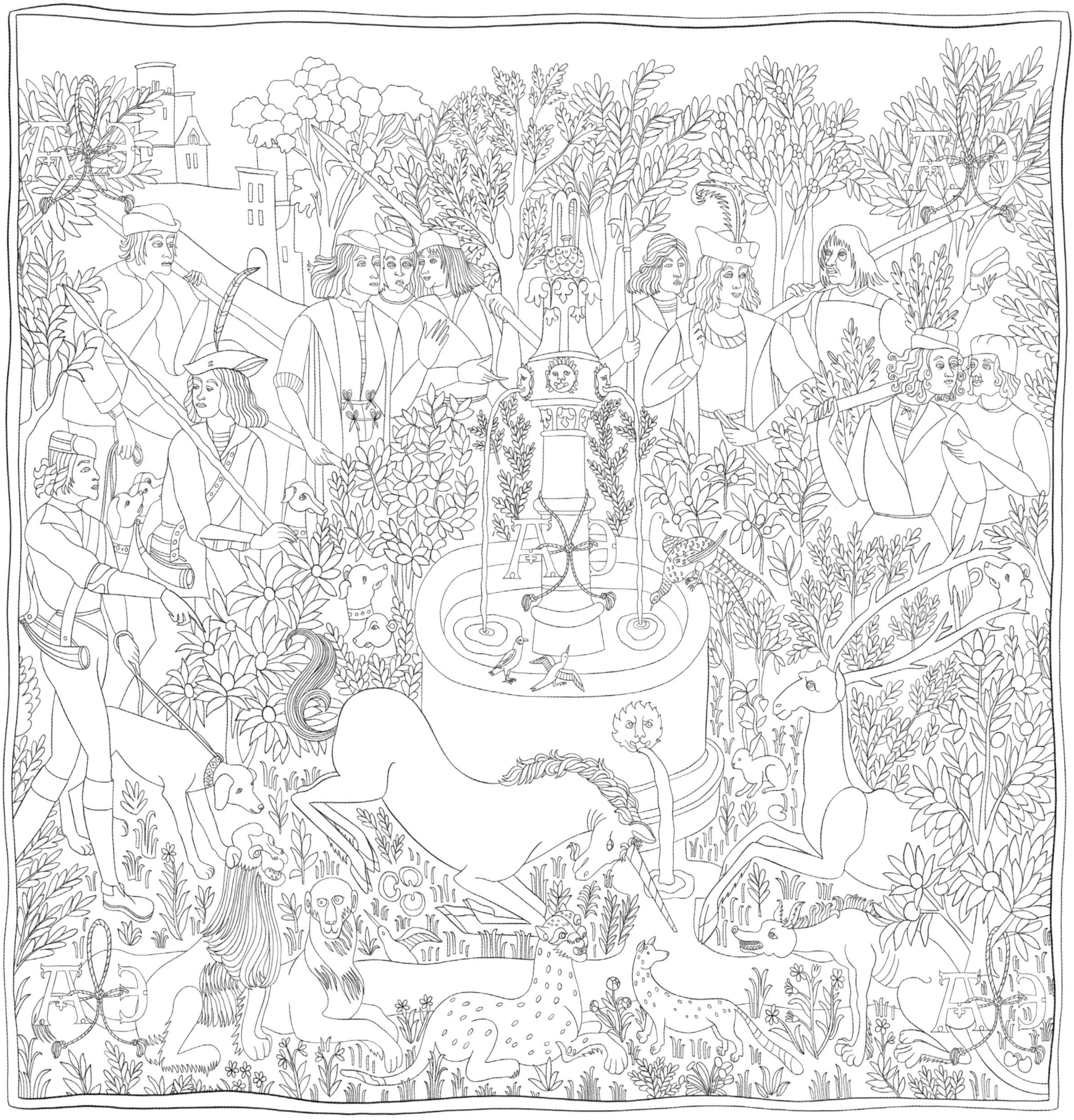

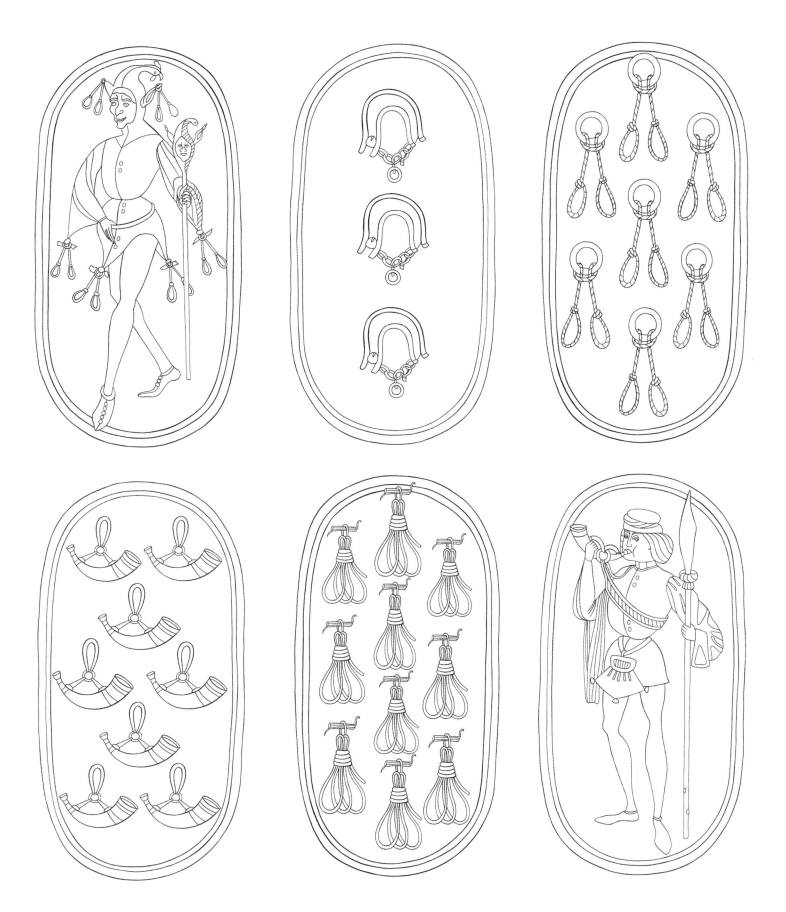

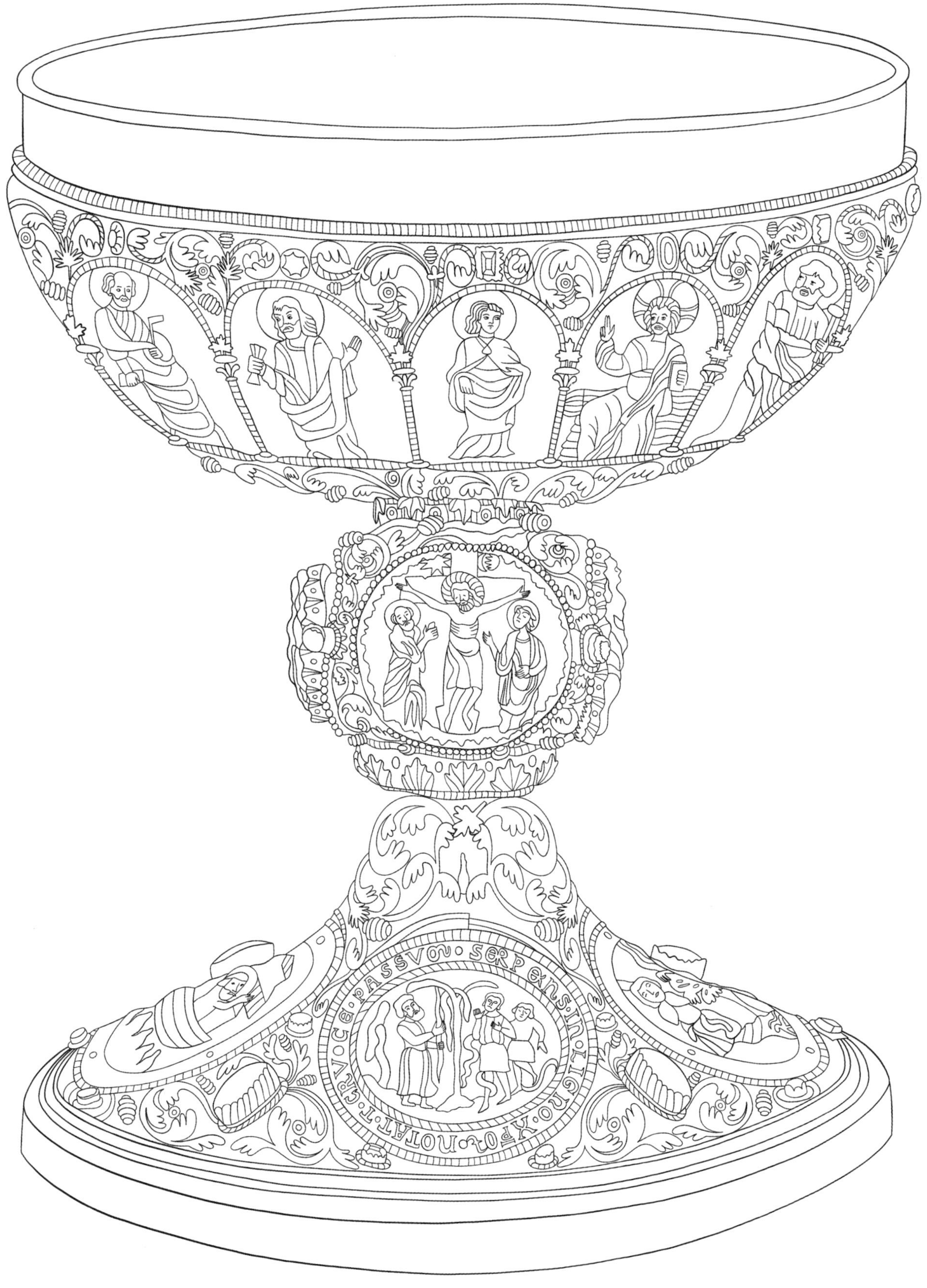

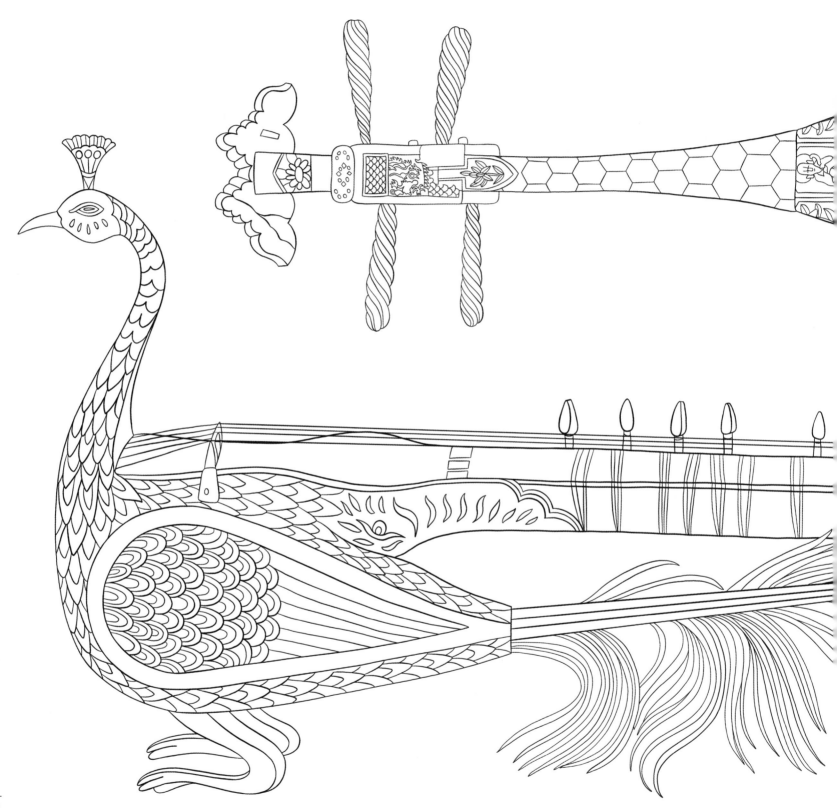

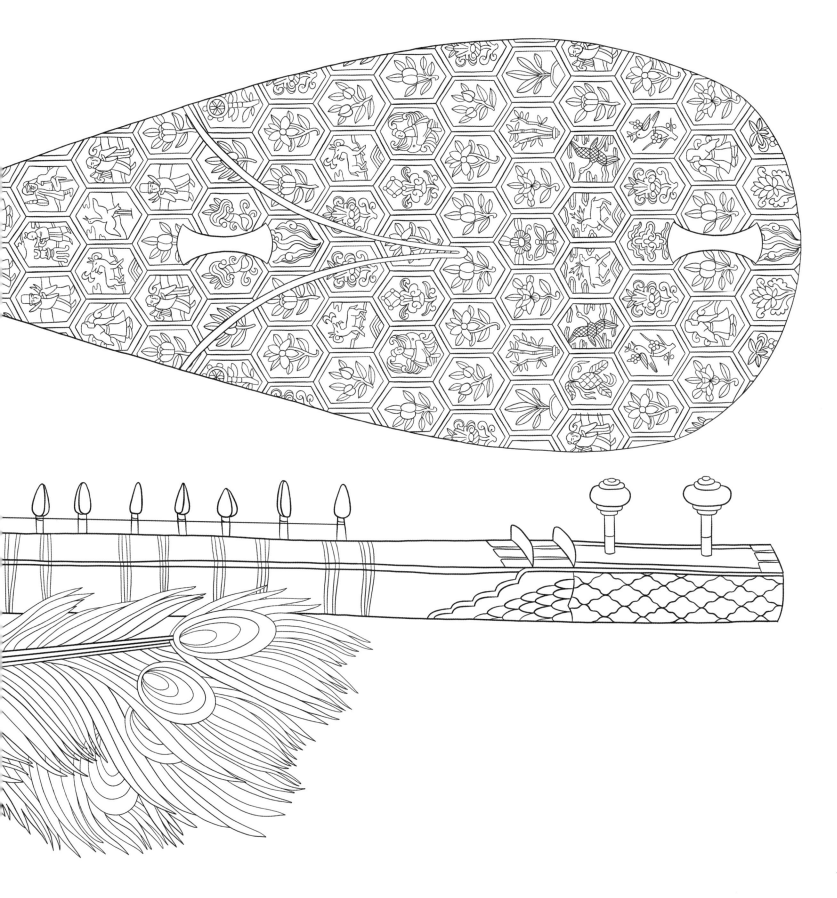

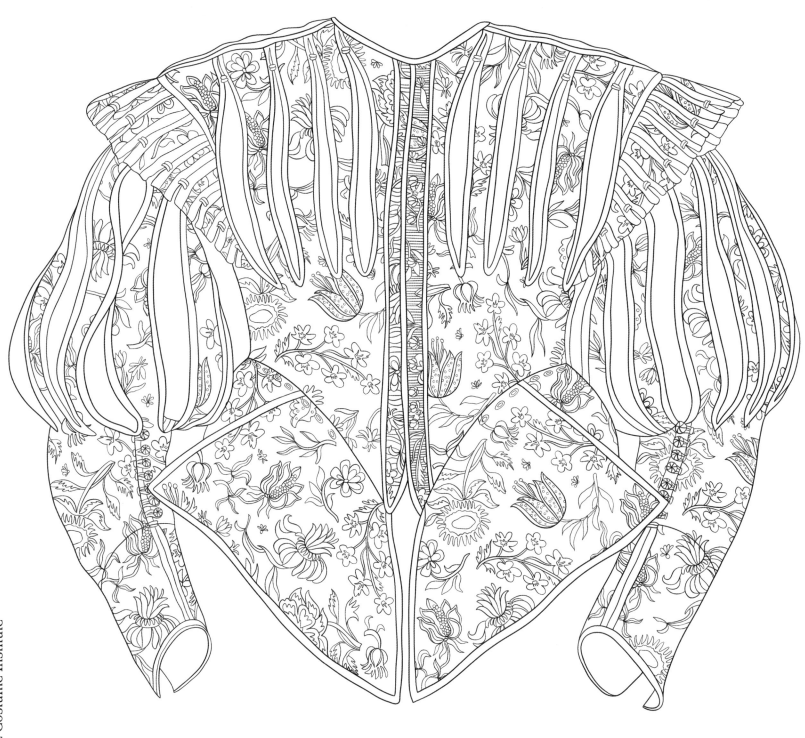

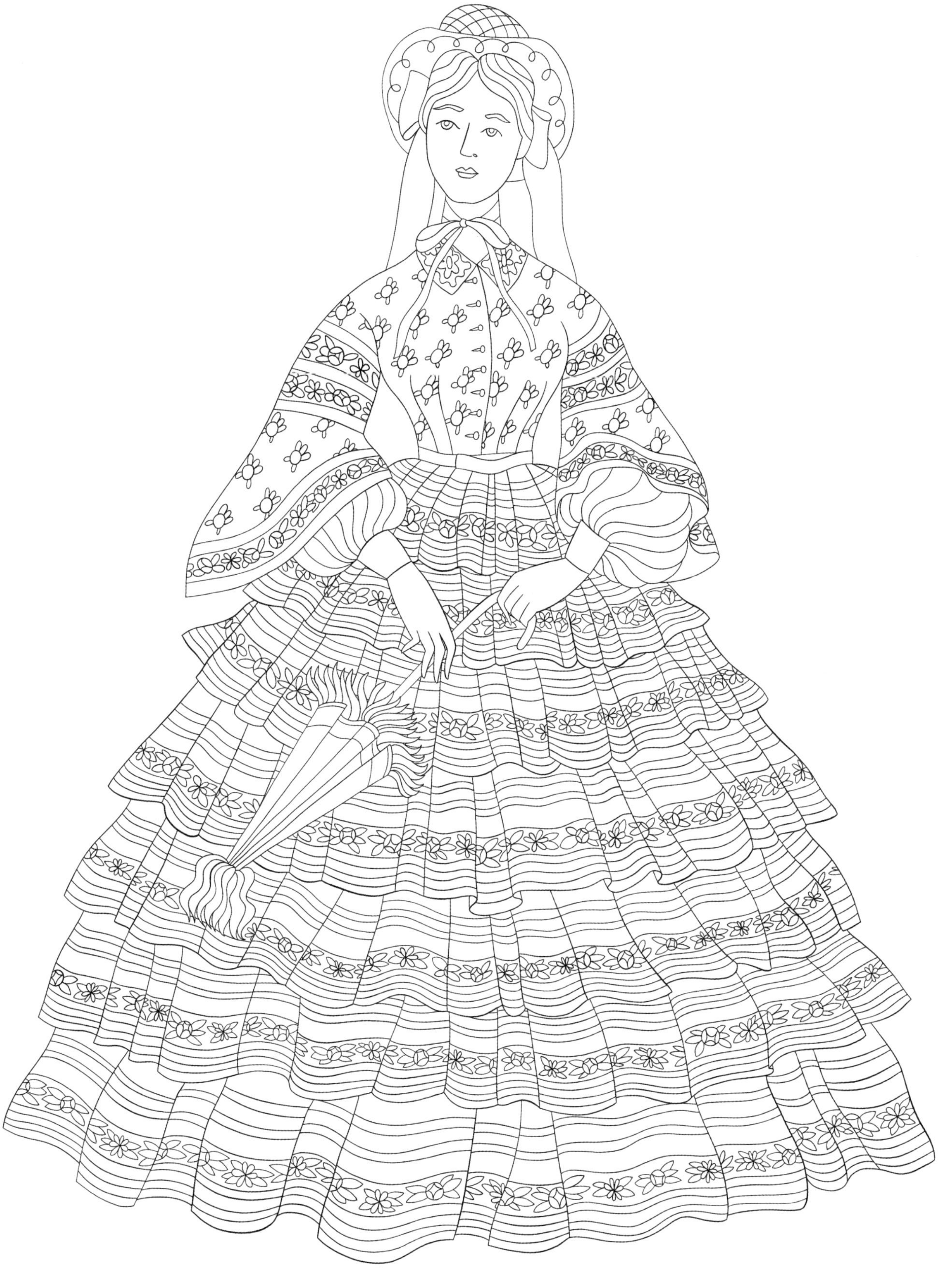

MME. GRAPANCHE
47 EAST 19TH ST.
NEW YORK

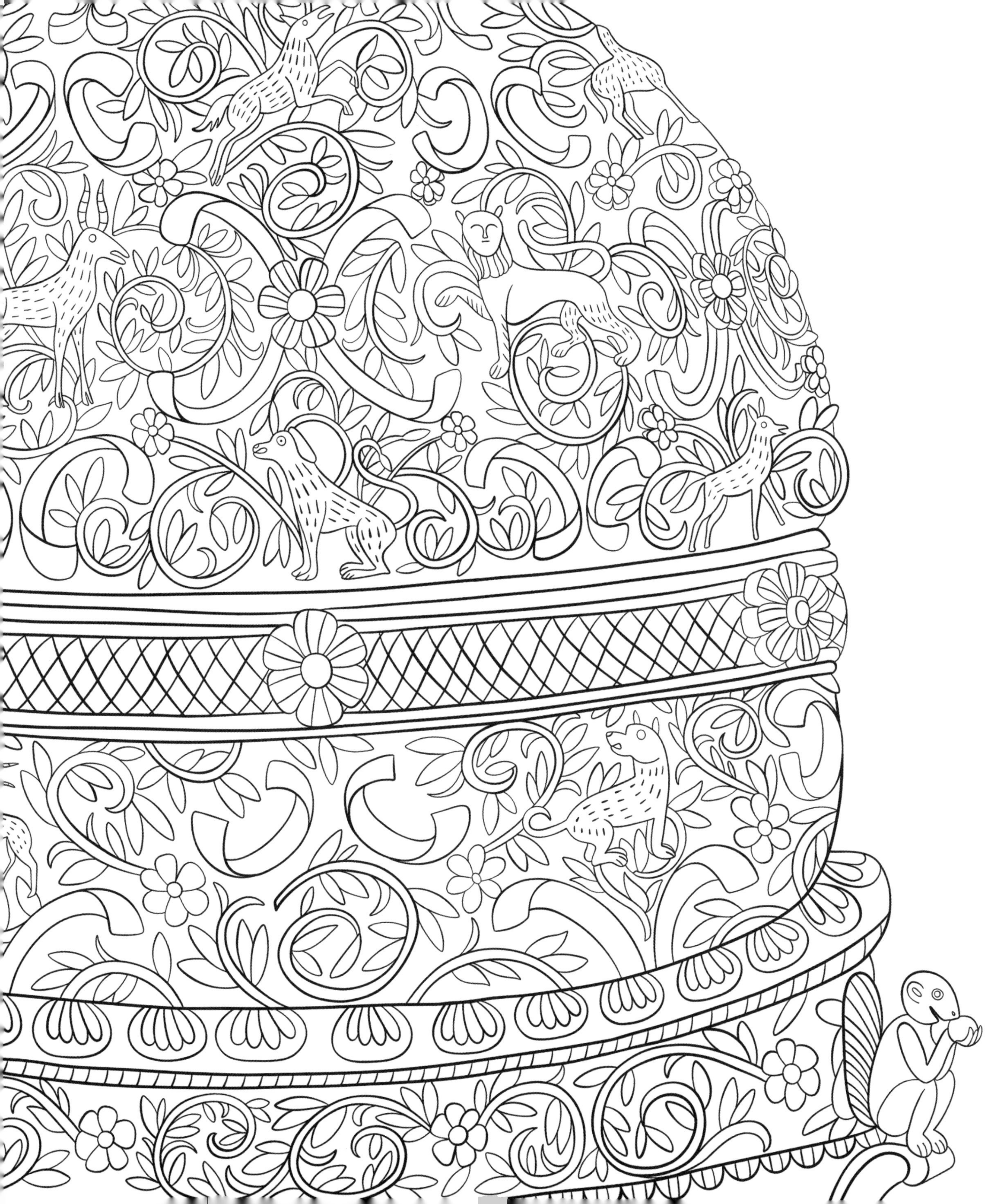

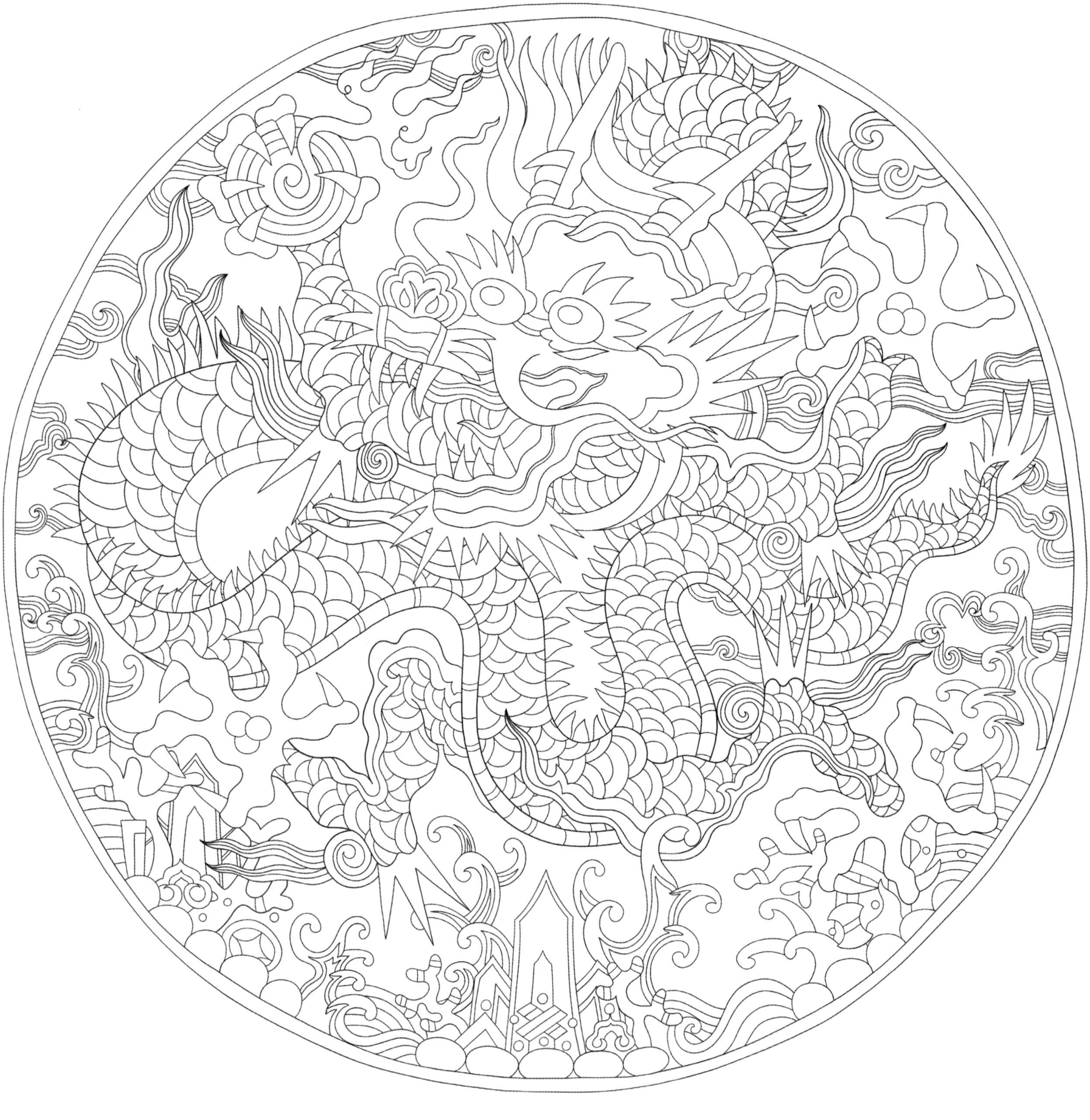

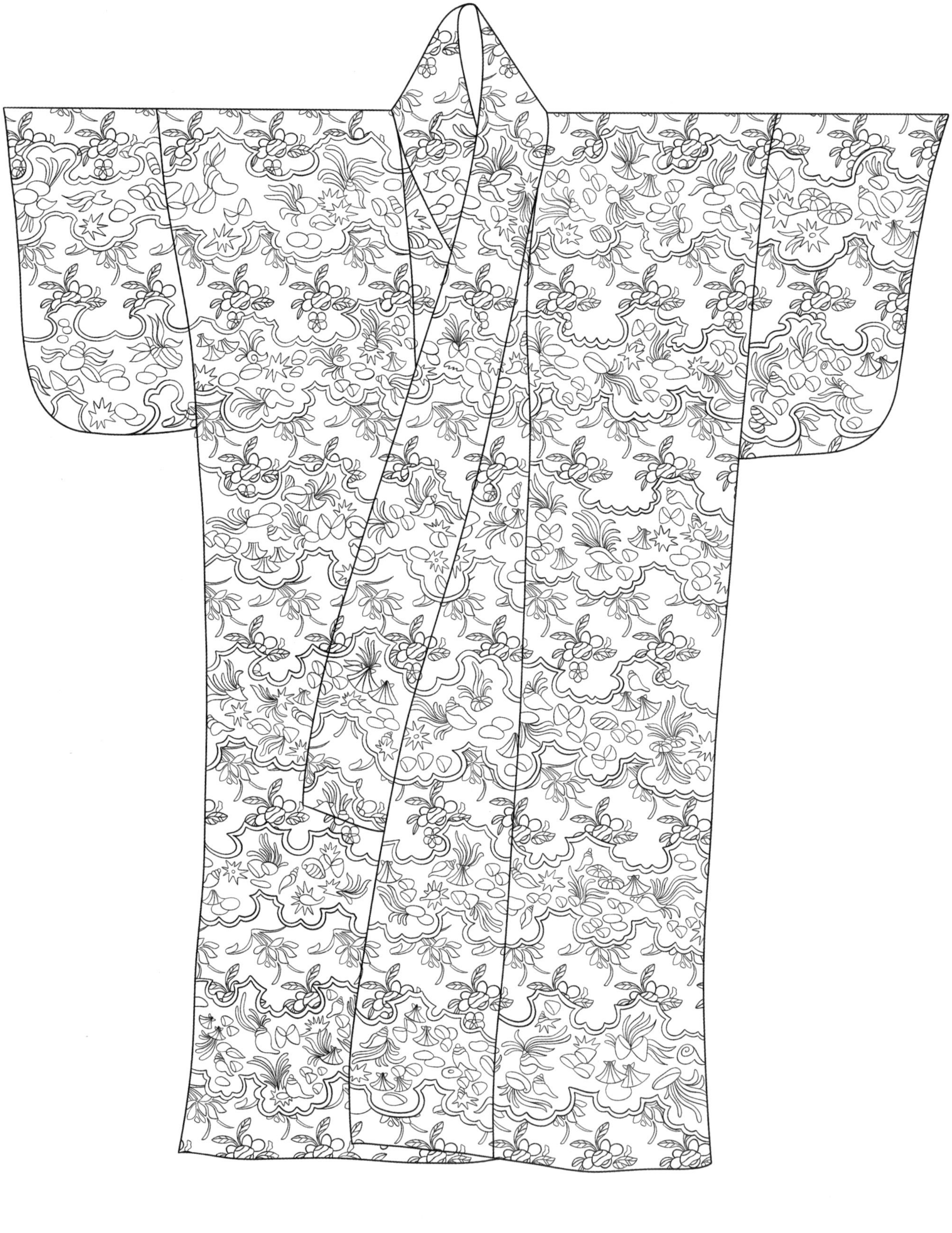

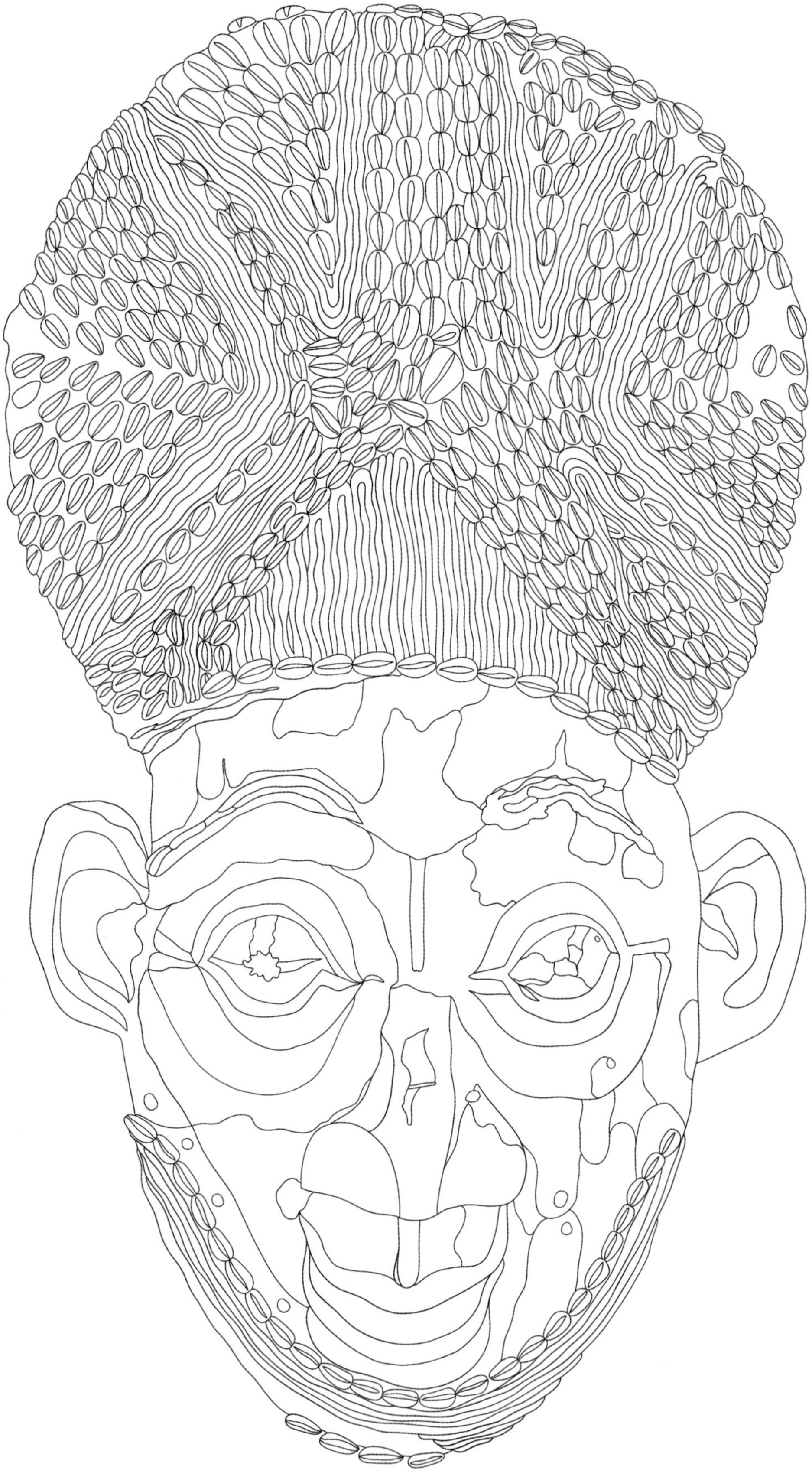

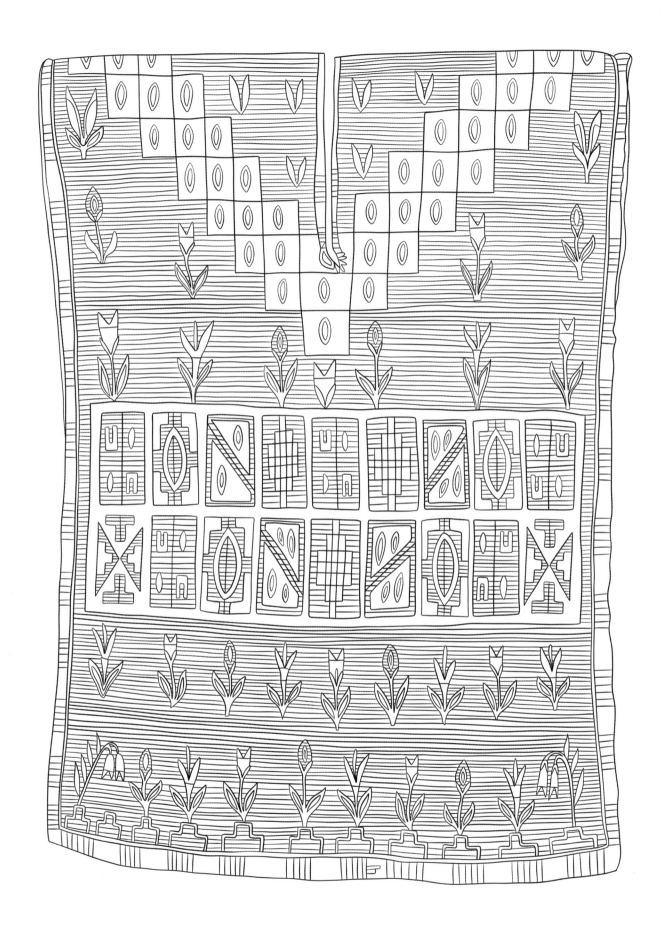

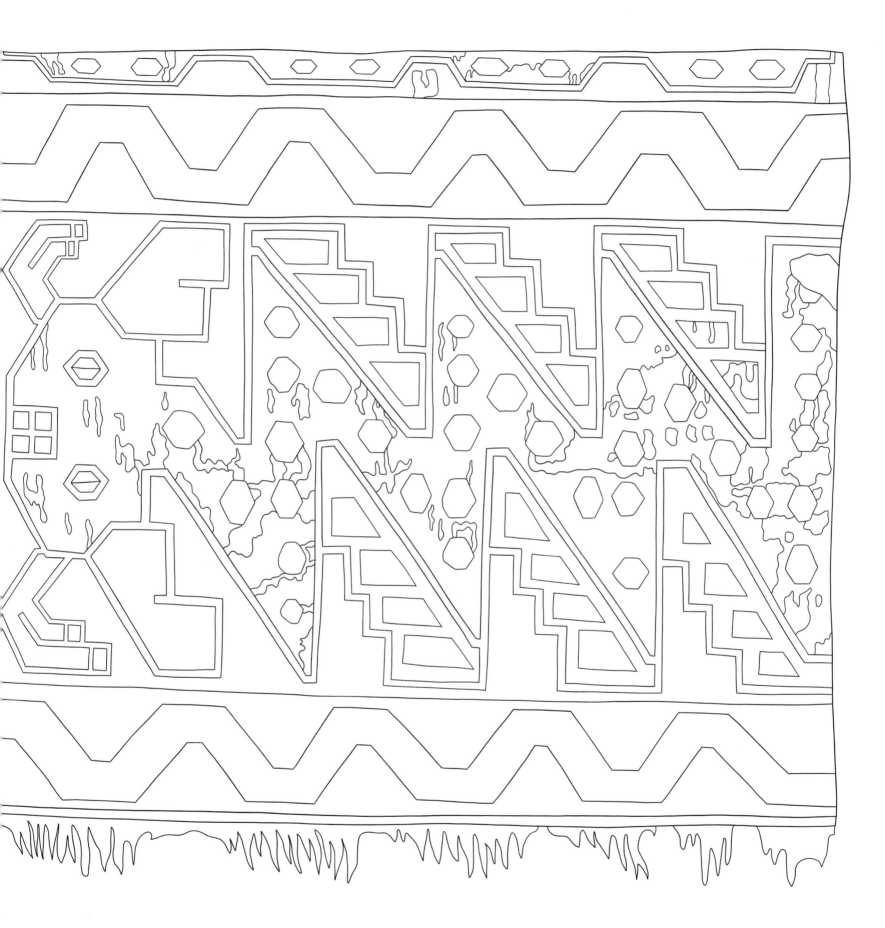

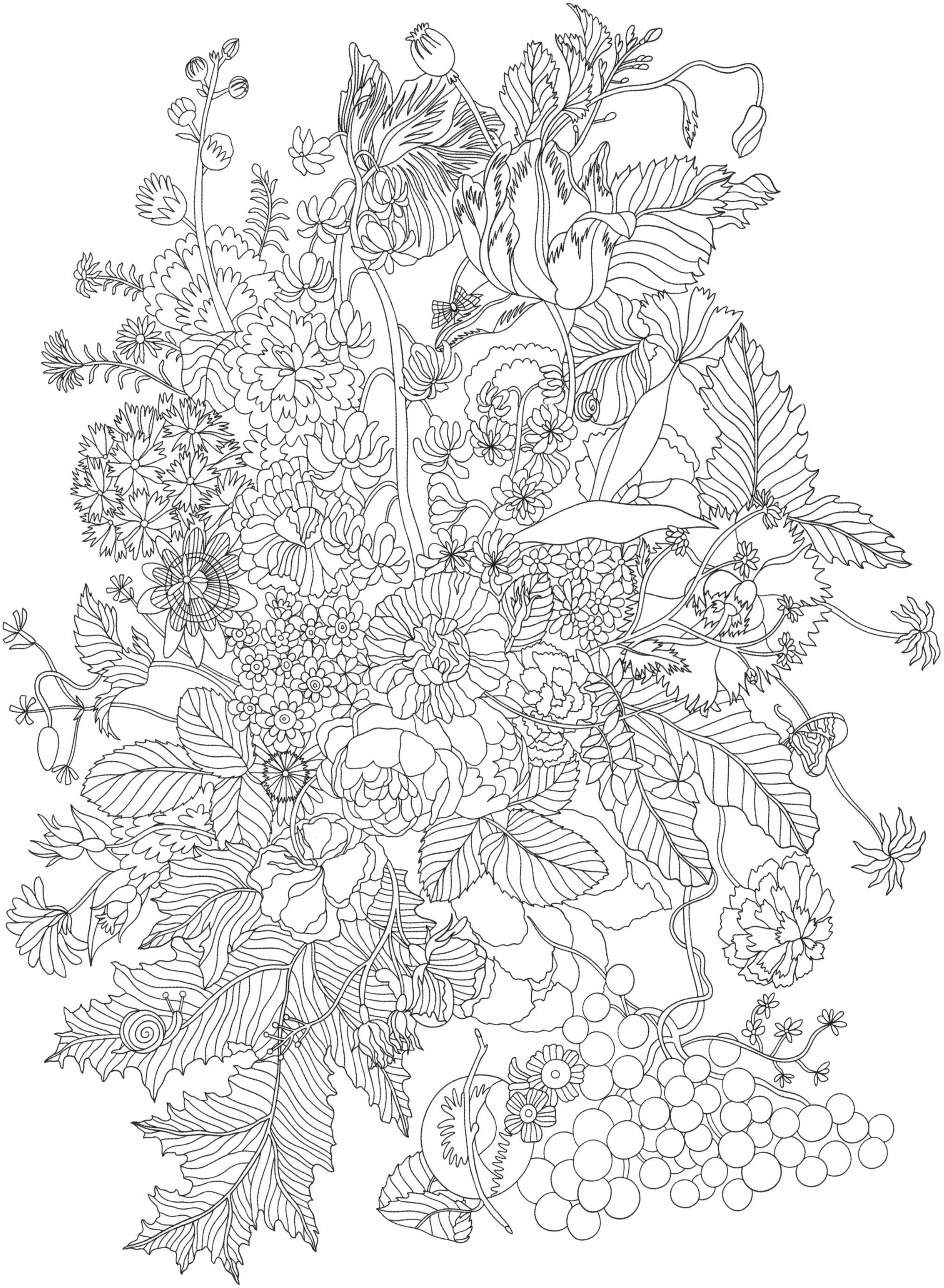

Now that you've colored the treasures of the Met Museum,
draw and color your own incredible treasures.

The illustrations in this book are inspired by real objects from the collection of The Metropolitan Museum of Art.

Page 6: Inlay Depicting "Horus of Gold" (4th century BCE). Ancient Egypt.

Page 4: Reconstruction of geometric decoration (1390–1352 BCE). Ancient Egypt.

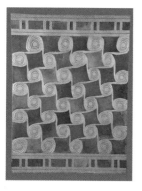

Page 5: Composite drawn from The King with Anubis, Tomb of Haremhab (1910–11 copy of 1323–1295 BCE original). Ancient Egypt.

Page 8-9: Coffin of Khnumnakht (1850–1750 BCE). Ancient Egypt.

Page 7: Sphinx of Hatshepsut. Ancient Egypt.

Page 10-11: Terracotta volute-krater (bowl for mixing wine and water), (450 BCE). Ancient Greece.

Page 12: Bronze helmet (late 7th century BCE). Ancient Greece, Cretan.

Page 14: Elements of an Italian Light-Cavalry Armor (c.1510).

Page 16: Mask by Muneakira (1745). Japan.

Page 13: Bronze helmet (late 7th BCE). Ancient Greece, Cretan.

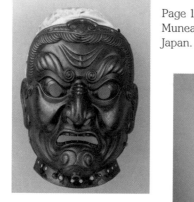

Page 18-19: image drawn from "The Album of Tournaments and Parades in Nuremberg" (16th–17th century). Germany.

Page 15: Armor garniture of George Clifford, Third Earl of Cumberland (1586). Britain.

Page 20: Armor for Man and Horse (1548). Germany.

Page 17: Armor by Muneakira (armor, 1717; helmet, late 16th century). Japan.

Page 21: Armor of Henry II, King of France (c.1555). France.

Page 22: Armor by Tomogotsu (18th century). Japan.

Page 23: Costume armor in the classical style (c.1788–90). France.

Page 25: *The Unicorn is Found* tapestry (1495–1505). Netherlands.

Page 26-27: Set of fifty-two playing cards (c.1475–80). Netherlands.

Page 28: Adoration of the Magi from seven scenes from the life of Christ (c.1390). Austria.

Page 24: *The Unicorn Rests in a Garden* tapestry (1495–1505). Netherlands.

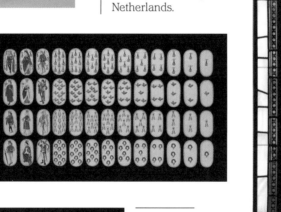

Page 29: Chalice (c.1230–50). Germany.

Page 32-33: Doublet and detail of doublet (early 1620s). France.

Page 34: Dress (1760). Britain.

Page 30-31: Pipa (16th–17th century). China.

Page 30-31: Taus (19th century). India.

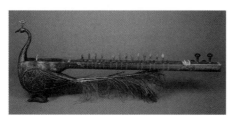

Page 35: Dress (c.1870). Britain.

Page 36: Shoes (1690–1700). France.

Page 37: Ensemble (c.1855). America/Europe.

Page 39: House of Worth Ball gown (c.1872). France.

Page 40: Suit (1774–92). France.

Page 38: Fan (mid-19th century). America/Europe.

Page 41: Madame Grapanche dinner dress and maker's label (1884–86). America.

Page 42-43: *Garden Gathering* (1640–50). Iran.

Page 46-47: Gold case for a Goa stone (17th–18th century). India.

Page 44-45: Royal Horse and Runner (16th–17th century). India.

Page 48: Pair of minbar doors (c.1325–30). Egypt.

Page 49: Star of Bethlehem quilt (c.1845). America.

Page 50: *Three Noblemen in Procession on an Elephant* (c.1790). India.

Page 51: Bowl with winged horse (12th century). Iran.

Page 54-55: Robe (kosode) with shells and sea grasses, (17th century). Japan.

Page 56: *Woman Admiring Plum Blossoms at Night* by Suzuki Harunobu (1725–1770). Japan.

Page 52: Dragon medallion (16th century). China.

Page 53: Pair of lions, Qing dynasty (1644–1911), Qianlong period (1736–95). China.

Page 57: Head of Bhairava (16th century). Nepal.

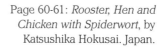

Page 58-59: *Under the Wave off Kanagawa*, also known as *The Great Wave*, by Katsushika Hokusai (c.1830–32). Japan.

Page 60-61: *Rooster, Hen and Chicken with Spiderwort*, by Katsushika Hokusai. Japan.

Page 62: Helmet mask (before 1880). Bamun kingdom.

Page 63: Panel ornaments for ceremonial sword and sheath (udamalore), (19th–20th century). Yoruba.

Page 64: Miniature tabard (1600–1700). Inca and Spanish.

Page 66-67: Tunic with confronting catfish (800–850). Peru.

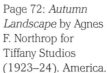

Page 68-69: Details from a boudoir in the Hôtel de Crillon (c.1777–80). France.

Page 63: Eagle relief (10th–13th century). Toltec.

Page 72: *Autumn Landscape* by Agnes F. Northrop for Tiffany Studios (1923–24). America.

Page 70: *Still Life with Apples and a Pot of Primroses* by Paul Cézanne (c.1890). France.

Page 71: *A Vase of Flowers* by Margareta Haverman (1716). Netherlands.

Page 73: *Hibiscus and Parrots* by Louis Comfort Tiffany for Tiffany Studios (c1910–12). America.

Acknowledgments:

DK would like to thank Rachel High, Leanne Graeff, and Morgan Pearce at The Met; Hilary Becker; and Lisa Silverman Meyers.

The publisher would like to thank The Metropolitan Museum of Art for their kind permission to reproduce and illustrate works of art from their collection.